mythic woods

mythic woods

The world's most remarkable forests

JONATHAN ROBERTS

Foreword by Thomas Pakenham

WEIDENFELD & NICOLSON

Contents

Foreword

Pliny, the great Roman naturalist, put it in three words: *Luci et silentia.* 'The groves and their silences'. He was explaining that primitive men used to dedicate to a god some particular tree that was especially tall, but now sophisticated Romans like himself 'worshipped the groves and their silences as much as statues shining with gold and ivory'.

I think I know what Pliny meant (although I'm primitive enough myself to pay homage to a beautiful tree with a hug). Woods and forests give many people today a form of religious experience, as it's there that you can celebrate a kind of compact with nature. A wood embraces you like the walls of a church. There are shafts of light from high windows, soaring sculptured columns, the tang of resin as sweet as incense – and the therapy of silence.

Sadly, as Jonathan Roberts makes clear in this eloquent book, silence is hard to come by these days even in the remote forest. Everywhere you hear the triumphant hymn of the chainsaw. A Douglas fir on Canada's Pacific coast takes 500 years to reach maturity. It can be cut down in five minutes and before long it's a truck load of logs heading the for the pulp mill or lumber yard. On Vancouver Island a juggernaut is not a homely metaphor. It's a logger's truck weighing 100 tons which takes the whole width of the road. In the Styx River valley, Tasmania, they use napalm on the trees after they've stripped out the best logs.

Previous pages: Lakeside pine forest in the Mt Assiniboine Provincial Park, British Columbia, Canada.

It's the cheapest way to clean the ground ready for the new crop.

What hope is there that our grandchildren will see the world's great forests that still survive today? Small hope, if you go by the statistics. Eighty-six per cent of the old growth forests of northern European Russia, and ninety per cent of the cloud forests of the Andes have vanished to feed the lumber mills. In thirty years an area the size of Europe has been hacked from the Amazonian rainforest to make grazing for cattle. At the same time a new danger to us all has been identified: global warming. Our planet's climate seems to be spinning out of control. Yet the antidote is well known. Burn less of the fossil fuels that release carbon and create poisonous greenhouse gases. Stop destroying the forests that soak up the carbon.

The new perception of eco-doom – the talk of floods that would flush New York into the Atlantic and heat that would fry Paris to a frazzle – may not have a bad result. It sends a ripple of fear down the spines of people unmoved by the thought of baobabs desecrated in Madagascar or tree frogs lost from Sumatra. Of course it will cost a great deal of money to save old growth forests from the chainsaw. But we may not have much choice. Perhaps we shall eventually say, thank heavens for global warming. As Voltaire might have put it, if global warming didn't exist it would need to be invented.

Introduction

This book is a celebration of fifteen woods or forests, chosen more or less at random from around the world. Some are big (the Russian Taiga, the Brazilian rainforest and Canada's Great Bear); others small (the Black Wood of Rannoch); one (Sherwood, perhaps the most famous of all) not even a forest in the modern sense of the word. But they all have in common a kind of ancient secrecy and sequestration that excites the fancy. They are mythic woods.

I wanted to write this book without, as it were, donning environmental overalls. The eco-clichés of our time – greenhouse gases, global warming, lungs of the earth, carbon sinks – were to be left lying in the grass. Nature, I thought and still think, has a way of springing its own surprises. But as my research and writing progressed, I became increasingly impressed, from example after example of threatened old-growth woodland, by the fact that one of the most vicious instruments ever invented by man is the petrol-driven chainsaw. Trees can barely keep up with axes. With chainsaws they do not stand a chance. A thousand years a-growing destroyed by fifteen minutes with a chainsaw: away to the mills on a lorry; a huge heap of woodchips; and a bundle of newsprint for the tabloids.

I dedicate this book to my new grandson, Max, in the hope that, when he is my age, the mythic woods and forests that I write about will still be there for him to visit and admire.

Amazon Rainforest

Opposite: Flooded forest on the Rio Negro, a major tributary of the Amazon and approximately 1,400 miles long. The vast rainforest it traverses covers over 2.3 million square miles.

The best way to see the lowland rainforest of Amazonia is to hitch a ride in a light aeroplane or in the gondola of a hot-air balloon and fly low over its canopy. The plain beneath is flat, at most undulating, and apparently thick-planted to the horizon with gigantic cauliflowers. Higher trees ('emergents') stick out at intervals like weeds, every now and then punctuating the green immensity with blooms of yellow, pink or purple. A river is a silver slash. The towering, slim-trunked emergents soar up to 200 feet from the forest floor. The tallest emergent ever recorded was one-third higher than Nelson's Column in London's Trafalgar Square: a giant 270-foot *Koompassia excelsa* from Sarawak.

The canopy beneath the emergents is an evergreen tangle of leaves and branches, vines, lianas and epiphytes (plants which grown on other plants), and grows at a level between about 65 and 100 feet above the forest floor. It is here that most of the bird, animal and reptile life in the forest occurs: a monkey highway, a stinkbird colony, a cat-eyed snake wrapped around a branch and on the lookout for a meal.

Left: A haze produced by intense evaporation in the early morning. Some 50 per cent of Amazonian rainfall consists of water previously evaporated from the forest floor.

The fringes of the forest, if you try and walk in from, say, a river bank, are a sunlit jungle of smaller trees, lianas, shrubs and herbaceous plants that recall sweating explorers and slashing cutlasses. Do not be deceived. Proceed farther, and the interior, below the sunlit canopy on the forest floor, is intimidatingly dark, silent and windless, like the nave of a Romanesque cathedral. It is also very hot and humid. Mosquitoes and biting insects swarm around exposed flesh. Underfoot it is bare, apart from dead, wet leaves, the odd shade-tolerant herb and exposed buttress roots that trip you up. The sun rises in the morning and burns off the mist that blankets the canopy. It rains, a tropical power shower, in the afternoon all the year round, making the forest drip through the night. High above, the crowns of the trees fit together like a puzzle, with a 3-foot 'shy zone', which botanists cannot yet fully explain, separating crown from crown in the canopy. Very little sunlight gets through to the forest floor below. There have been few European foot-travellers through the Brazilian rainforest, from the first Portuguese explorers in the sixteenth century down to the present day, who have not admitted to the difficulties of sub-canopy navigation and to their relief upon getting out. One botanist became so frustrated trying, in the gloom, to identify Amazonian tree species from bare trunks – they can exceed eighty per acre – that he trained a monkey to climb up into the canopy to retrieve foliage and fruit.

You can still fly for many hours across some parts of Amazonia without seeing any human trace: no house, no road, no field. It is the largest tropical forest in the world, bigger than the whole of Europe. The Brazilian forest alone (which covers 60 per cent of the country) extends over a vast area, 2 million square miles, more than half the size of the continental United States. It extends into nine different countries and is the most species-rich environment on Earth, home to about one-fifth of the world's plants and birds, and one-tenth of all its mammals, including endangered celebrities like the giant otter and the jaguar. Much of it

Opposite: *Ceiba pentandra* is the tallest species of tree in the Amazon rainforest, growing to over 200 feet. These giants are held sacred in Mayan belief.

remains unexplored. New species, especially of insects, are reported almost every day.

There is another way into the rainforest, by boat; especially during the annual flooding of the Amazon basin, when the water level can rise 40 feet, partly or wholly submerging many trees and elevating the traveller that much nearer the canopy, where the action is. The trees do not seem to mind the water. Most keep their leaves, and some have learned to produce floating fruit that are eaten and distributed by swamp-dwelling fish like piranha and tambaqui. If you are out at night in a canoe, though, watch out for Great Snake (*cobra grande*). The Indians are terrified of it. A sort of supernatural game warden, it protects fish-spawning areas and makes the Loch Ness monster look like an earthworm: 250 yards long, with huge searchlight eyes set a yard apart. It likes junction pools, where tributaries join the great river, and the water that boils up from the bottom is an indication of its presence. *Cobra grande* can swallow a canoe, and its occupants, in one gulp.

In 1933 Peter Fleming wrote in *Brazilian Adventure*: 'It seemed to me that about a tenth of the interior of Brazil was perpetually in flames.' He was referring to the presence of forest Indians, who understood and respected their environment: their temporary patchworks of slash-and-burn agriculture were allowed, in time, to regenerate as rainforest. But in the mid-1970s Brazil's urban poor, issued by the government with free chainsaws and given access to the interior by new roads like the Trans-Amazon highway, embarked on a massacre without limits:

'a land without men for men without land'. The *queimada* (burning) seasons had begun with a vengeance. A hole in the rainforest the size of France was opened up, probably forever, to make way for cattle pasture, crops, roads and human settlements. In 1988 airports all over Brazil were closed for weeks because of smoke from the west. Scientists predicted rainforest extinction within fifty years.

In the twelve months prior to August 1995, 12,200 square miles of rainforest went up in smoke. After that, for the next six years, the situation seemed to improve, the annual rate of loss dropping to, and holding steady at, about 7,563 square miles, an area about the size of Wales. But in August 2002 satellite data from Brazil's National Institute for Space Research revealed that the annual figure had suddenly shot up again, by about 40 per cent, to 10,190 square miles. The reason? Huge demand in Europe and the Far East for soybeans, their export made even more profitable by a weak Brazilian currency. Faced with a choice between saving the rainforest and feeding and employing its urban poor, the left-wing government of President Luiz da Silva chose, in effect, the latter. In the next five to seven years Brazil is expected to overtake the United States as the world's top soy exporter, and to take a huge bite, in the process, out of its rainforest. Nearly one-fifth has already been consumed. The solution, of course, is money for conservation: lots of it and probably international. Brazil's paradox is that she lacks the short-term fiscal resources to protect and develop her most precious long-term asset, which also happens to be one of our planet's greatest treasures.

Overleaf: A capercaillie, a large game bird that populated the original Caledonian woodland. The species became extinct in Scotland in 1785 and was reintroduced again in 1837. It is once again facing extinction, having declined to less than 1,000 individuals.

Page 21: The largest and longest-lived tree in the Caledonian forest, the hardy Scots pine is the backbone of its ecosystem, supporting countless other species.

The Black Wood of Rannoch

'If one could have flown,' wrote J.G. Clark in 1952 in his *Prehistoric Europe*, 'over northern Europe during Mesolithic times [*c*.5,000 BC], it is doubtful whether more than an occasional wisp of smoke from some camp fire, or maybe a small cluster of huts or shelters by a river bank or old lake bed, would have advertised the presence of man: in all essentials the forest would have stretched unbroken, save only by mountain, swamp and water, to the margins of the sea.'

The Black Wood of Rannoch is a remnant of the ancient Caledonian forest that once covered much of the Highlands.

In the heart of Perthshire, at the east end of a high moor as desolate and solitary as anywhere to be found in Scotland, there persists a remnant of those Mesolithic, naturally regenerating, ancient Caledonian pines that once formed a continuous wildwood rug from Ireland to China, from Norway to Spain. Today, the Black Wood stretches for about four miles, a mile deep, along the south side of Loch Rannoch.

When the sun slants across the Highlands in the evening and lights up the summit of Schiehallion on the eastern horizon, the trunks of the Scots pines of the Black Wood glow orange-red; their canopies bluish green. Beneath them, from a carpet of purple heather, grows a mossy, fairy-tale tangle of birch and rowan, alder and juniper. In spring, wood anemones, orchids and violets are scattered across the forest floor. In prehistoric times this was a haunt of elk and wolf, lynx and brown bear; now foxes, badgers, weasels and stoats are their inheritors. There are occasional sightings of a rare pine marten, or wild cat. Crossbills, capercaillie and black game are pine-feeders, and live in the wood. Ten thousand years ago, when the glaciers of the last Ice Age retreated from the Highland glens, the first trees to colonise the moraines left in the wake of the ice's retreat were the birches. Scots pines, following hard behind over the continental land bridge that is now the southern North Sea, soon became established as a partner-species. Their seed cones found favourable niches among the decaying sphagnum mosses, sedges and cotton grass that were forming bogs in the hollows of the hills, and their seedlings prospered on the exposed mountainsides (especially the north-facing slopes where the competition with other species was less intense). The lower, more fertile, alkaline plains to the east and south of the Highland Fault were colonised by forests of oak and elm, with an under-storey of holly and hazel.

The Scots pine's tolerance of harsh conditions is beaten only by that of birch, which grows in a belt beyond the last pine in Norway. Scots pine has been known to survive winter temperatures as low as minus 83°F (minus 64°C) in Siberia. It shrugs off gales in the western Highlands, in an area where there are twenty to thirty gale-days per year. The highest altitude recorded for a native pine in Scotland is 2,800 feet on Ben Macdhui in the Cairngorms, northwest of Mar. The tree was only a stunted little thing, one foot high, but alive.

Native Scots pines tend to be long-lived. They resist the fungal diseases that their cultivar cousins are heir to (which is one of the reasons why their genetic inheritance should be preserved at all costs). Some trees in the Black Wood go back two hundred and fifty years, the oldest perhaps three hundred. The record for a living pine in Scotland is four hundred and fifty years. What has reduced the ancient Caledonian forest to its present Rorke's-Drift, last-ditch status? The impact, of course, of man.

Previous pages: A river
borders the remnants of
a once extensive, ancient
forest – the Black Wood
of Rannoch.

First to be eroded were the oak forests of the Lowlands. The land
was stripped for agriculture, the timber for house- and ship-building,
as fuel for smelter and hearth. Medieval law-makers did their best to
conserve the trees: they limited pigs and pannage (acorn-browsing),
goat-grazing and fire-raising in the oak forests. But the winds of economic
necessity were blowing against them. By the beginning of the seventeenth
century, nearly all the oaks were gone and Scotland had become an
importer of timber from Prussia and Denmark. Surveyors turned their
attention to the less accessible pine forests of the Highlands: the straight
trunks were good for planking and naval masts, and the faggots, with
their dribbling pine resin, made excellent flambeaux for lighting. But
how to get the timber out? Float it down the rivers. In the case of the
Black Wood, down a mile-long artificial sluice to Loch Rannoch, then
on down the Tummel to the Tay.

Between 1600 and 1850, nearly all the native pine woods of
Scotland were cut down. Grazing sheep and red deer – both partial to
pine seedlings – finished the job. Within 250 years the destruction was

complete: a paradigm of what might still happen, on a much larger scale, in Amazonia or northern Russia. The Black Wood was saved, probably, by being on the wrong side in the Jacobite Rebellion of 1745. Its owners, the Robertsons, who had fought and won for Robert Bruce at Bannockburn in 1314, and fought and lost for Charles Stuart at Culloden, ceded the wood in 1749 to the Commissioners of the Forfeited Estates, who looked after it with admirable efficiency. They enclosed it with ditch and dyke to keep out grazing animals, reduced felling, put pigs on the bare places to break up the ground, and dropped cones every two paces or so to release seed. Trees dating from their stewardship are still standing.

The Black Wood is not the only relic of the ancient forest that once clothed the Caledonian Highlands – there are other sites, on Speyside farther north for example, where stands of these wonderful old trees still persist. But it is one of the best preserved, within the Forestry Commission's Tay Forest Park, and most accessible. Today, it is a privilege, from the car park by the Carie Burn on the loch's southern shore, to wander off into the secret recesses of the Black Wood of Rannoch.

The Sundarban Mangrove Forests of the Ganges Delta

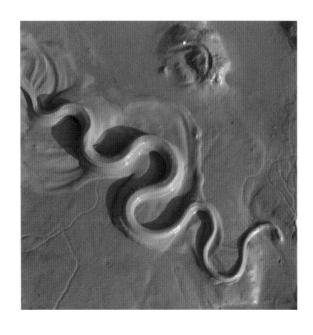

If you are unlucky enough to be stranded at low tide in the Sundarban mangroves of the Ganges Delta, the first thing you will notice is a ghastly smell: worse than decaying fish or rotten eggs. The smell is *sui generis,* a memorandum of all the debris swept down the Brahmaputra, Meghna and Ganges rivers, which, from time immemorial, have deposited their silts into this vast delta.

Page 30: A sea snake at low tide on a mud flat in the coastal area of the Sundarbans.

Page 31: A creek winding through the mangrove forest. The little clearing on the right was caused by woodcutters, who had piled up tree trunks here before they were loaded on a barge.

Right: The sinuous roots of the cedar or cannonball mangrove (*Xylocarpus granatum*) at low tide.

Look around you, if you can stand the stench. The swamp is a primordial, eerie place, hot and humid and silent except for the odd plop of a fiddler crab in the mud or the shriek of a gull. All botany, they say, began in the sea, and in this brackish limbo, halfway between sea and land, one can readily imagine seaweeds, whose elongated, wood-forming cells are able to make roots and branches and photosynthesising leaves, beginning their slow usurpation of the land.

The shrubs and trees that surround you (only a few feet high on the fringes, others up to 100 feet high in the interior) are very strange, very primitive. Their canopy reminds one of laurel, with its thick, leathery, evergreen leaves. Below, it is a different story. Some seem to stand in the mud on a spidery, arching network of stilt-like roots, like banyan trees; others push up aerial rootlets, which botanists call 'pneumatophores', around them like a battery of miniature organ pipes.

That is the way they breathe. The salty mud is anaerobic, and the roots get their oxygen, when the tide is out, directly from the air through cork-like pores in their bark. In mangrove forests, the silt level is forever rising and the mangroves keep pace by growing breathing roots at successively higher levels. Non-breathing roots pierce deep into the shifting silt for anchorage against the tides, which, at their highest, can reach the level of their leaves.

One of the most common species in the Sundarbans, the red mangrove (*Rhizophera apiculata*), has evolved a clever method of reproducing itself in the fast-flowing tides. Its seed germinates while still attached to the parent and grows a mud-piercing, arrow-like rootlet about one foot long, which buries itself in the silt beneath when it falls off the parent tree.

The Sundarban mangroves are technically rainforests, in the sense that they receive more than 80 inches of rain throughout the year. The term 'tropical rainforest', thus defined, was first invented by a German botanist called A.F.W. Schimper in 1898. The Sundarbans cover a vast coastal area: more than 3,800 square miles straddling the border of India with Bangladesh. They are the most extensive mangrove forests in the world. You might expect, because of their inaccessible and alien nature, that they would be unaffected by the ravages of man. Not so. Bangladesh, one of the most populous countries on this planet, has destroyed 95 per cent of its original monsoon- and rainforest, including its mangroves, and species such as swamp deer, nilgai (grey antelope) and the great Indian rhinoceros are now extinct within its territory. The Royal Bengal tiger hangs on in the eastern Sundarbans, in a reserve created in 1973 and now a UNESCO World Heritage Site. There were 270 of them at the last count; magnificent creatures that have adapted to life in the swamps. They swim like eels, eat fish, and are unafraid of the crocodiles (which can be up to 26 feet long and are known locally as 'salties'), with whom they share their inhospitable environment.

Mangrove wood (*Rhizophora* timber), suffers from the advantages of being hard and durable, close-grained, water- and mollusc-resistant, and an attractive reddish-brown colour. In other words, it is good for house-building, pit props, fencing, firewood, charcoal and (especially) wood pulp, new supplies of which paper companies from Japan are forever on the lookout for. The mangroves of the Philippine islands have long since vanished, having been cleared to make ponds for prawn- and fish-farming. Sundari trees (*Heritiera fomes*), once dominant among the mangroves of the Ganges Delta, are rarities now, victims of illegal felling.

If you are in the Sundarbans, the best way to see the Royal Bengal tigers is to hire a rowing boat and boatman from, say, Sajnakhali. He will paddle you quietly along the maze of creeks and waterways, without scaring the wildlife as the tourist motorboats do. You may see a tigress on a mud bank teaching her cubs to swim: a private moment within this remarkable mangrove rainforest that bestrides both land and sea.

A Bengal tiger crossing one of the numerous small creeks. Over fifty people a year are killed by tigers in the Sundarbans.

*Cloud Forests of
the Andes*

If you travel west along the equator, out of the lowland rainforest of Brazil and up into the cordilleras of the Andes, you will encounter, as you climb into the clouds, a waterlogged world of peat and moss, ferns and lichens, gnarled and dripping trees. Visibility, because of the constant fog, is down to a few yards; light levels, above and below the evergreen canopy, are very low. The wind blows harder and colder for every yard that you ascend. It is like climbing vertically out of a sauna. You will soon be fishing in your rucksack for rainwear, fleece waistcoat and woolly hat.

Page 40: The rare spectacled bear is variously treated in Andean mythology. In some cultures, the bear is revered as a god; in others, it is regarded as evil and destroyed. They are listed as vulnerable and still hunted for sport and culled by farmers.

Page 42: Pathways through the forest: animals, especially monkeys and sloths, use slow-growing liana vines to move between the canopy and the forest floor. Thick lianas are the only sure sign of old-growth rainforest.

Opposite: *Cecropia* trees (related to stinging nettles) provide a climbing-frame for mosses, lianas, orchids and fungi.

You have entered the cloud forests, the *cejas de las montañas*, as the Spanish call them, the 'eyebrows of the mountains'. They form a narrow, curving, disjointed ribbon down the high spine of South America, from Panama to Argentina: a cold and watery garland for the sweating brow of the Amazonian floodplains to the east below.

Here the mighty condor, with a wingspan of almost 10 feet, makes circles among the peaks. In the forest, you might, if you are lucky, catch a glimpse of a spectacled bear (*Tremarctos ornatus*), South America's only native (and highly endangered) bear, with white fur patches around its eyes; or disturb a tapir, a shy nocturnal creature the size of a large pig, with a trunk for a snout; or listen to the wails of bearded howler monkeys.

In the tropics, for every 1,000 feet you climb, the temperature drops by between one and two degrees centigrade. The cloud forests begin at about 6,000 feet and extend as high as 12,500 feet. At lower levels the trees, from 50 to 65 feet high, tend to be twisted and multi-stemmed (the quick-growing *Cecropia*, for example, of the *Urticaceae*, or nettle, family), quite unlike the straight-trunked giants left behind in the Amazonian floodplain. Many resemble temperate species like oak, beech and laurel. They are bearded with mosses and draped with lianas and epiphytes. Bright-coloured orchids grow as if out of the air; tree ferns float like parasols; fungi are everywhere. You might be in some demented, abandoned woodland garden on a wet Wednesday in Ireland.

Opposite: Cloud forests are shrouded in mist all year long.

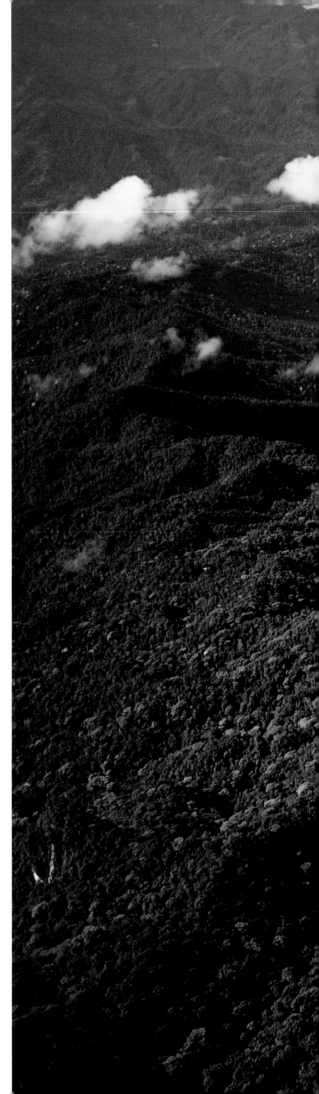

At high altitudes, in the bitter-cold winds, the trees are barely the height of a man, and covered in moss. The quenual tree, found at nearly 16,000 feet in the Peruvian Andes, holds the world arboreal record for growing at extreme altitudes; it resembles a gnarled old blackthorn in an English hedgerow.

The function of the mountain trees, which have smaller, narrower, more leathery leaves than those in the rainforest lowlands, is to strip water from the clouds and drip-feed it to the boggy ground beneath, where the humus and peat act as a filtering, water-retentive sponge – a vast Andean reservoir – for the myriad streams that feed down into the Amazon basin. If the trees are degraded, the high rainfall – up to 400 inches in some places – washes away the ground-cover and brings the rivers down in catastrophic, silt-laden flood.

Right: Foothills of the Andes in western Ecuador. The sloping landscape allows the sun's rays to penetrate deep inside the dense forest, creating an eco-system that is home to many unique life forms.

Which is exactly what is happening, at an alarming pace. Scientists, on the evidence of satellite photographs, have warned that 90 per cent of the cloud forests of the northern Andes have already gone and the rest could be destroyed in a decade unless something is done to stop the clear-cutting of the mountainsides for fuel, cattle grazing and coca plantations. The pity of it is that we know so little about the intricate ecosystems and niche habitats that the forests support. There are only a handful of scientists working up there in the mist. Percy Nuñez, a biologist with a passion for cloud forests, has collected up to 40,000 plants in southern Peru. He believes that he has only just scratched the surface, that four-fifths of the species – both plants and animals – endemic to the mountains have never even been catalogued by science. A small area of the cordilleras can furnish as many plant species, he says, as the whole continent of Europe.

The forest Indians of South America believe in a goblin who punishes those who abuse Nature. They call it *curupira*, the father of game. It is small, hairy and runt-like, with feet turned backwards. It lives in headwater forests and protects animals like white-lipped peccaries (a pig-like creature) and deer, on whose heads it sometimes rides around. If an Indian kills too many peccaries at one go, or wastefully cuts down a tree, *curupira* whistles him into the dark woods, to his death. We should beware lest our own and future generations of man are whistled away to oblivion.

Opposite: Aerial roots. Andean cloud forests tend to grow on poor, nutrient-depleted soils, and trees are prepared to put out roots almost anywhere in search of extra food.

Blue Cedar Forests of the Atlas

When he was an old man in the years after the First World War, Louis-Hubert Lyautey, Maréchal de France, was given a retirement job as Resident General of Morocco under the French protectorate. Someone told him that the Moroccan Atlas mountain range, which stretches from Agadir to the Mediterranean, had once been covered by a cedar forest. He ordered it replanted at once. His civil servants objected that such old-growth forests took millennia to establish. Lyautey replied briskly: 'That, gentlemen, is why we shall start immediately.'

Previous pages: Cedar cone and fully grown tree. The genus *Cedrus*, from the ancient Greek *kedros*, consists of three species of true cedar, all prevalent in the Old World.

Opposite: A seedling breaks through the arid plateau of the High Atlas. If it survives, it may live for 500 years.

If you drive south from Fez on the Route Principale 24 you will enter, after a couple of hours, the limestone foothills of the Middle Atlas mountains, the first of the three great barrier-walls (the others are the High Atlas and the Anti-Atlas beyond it) that separate Morocco and Algeria from the world's hottest and biggest desert some 125 miles away to the south. Here, on the north side of the mountains, between about 4,000 and 7,000 feet, there still grow remnants of the old-growth, high-altitude cedar forests that once carpeted the Atlas from end to end. From the mountain town of Azrou, up and over the high pass of Tizi-n-Tretten (6,800 feet), you can walk all day in the cedar-scented shade of these wonderful old trees, along precipitous paths that skirt sounding waterfalls and bubbling springs. Go early in the year, before the heat of summer burns the mountains to dust, and as you pass through an under-storey of oak and juniper, your way will be strewn with spring flowers: violets, primroses, anemones, cyclamen, celandine, pheasant's eye narcissus. The higher you climb, the taller the cedars grow – up to 120 feet – and the wider they cast their shade. As you gain the pass, you will confront across an arid plateau the snowy mountain tops of the High Atlas, salmon-pink in the sunshine; there you can catch a whiff of the sweet, thick smell of the Sahara.

The Atlas cedar (*Cedrus atlantica*), is one of only three true species of cedar. Differentiating the species is not always an easy task. As a rough rule of thumb, the side branches of *atlantica* tend to ascend from the trunk, while those of its close relative, the cedar of Lebanon (*C. libani*) – which Solomon used to build his temple and which now survives in Lebanon only in sad fragments – grow out horizontally. The Deodar cedar (*C. deodara*), which still grows wild in Afghanistan and the western Himalayas, has branches that descend. The cedar of Lebanon has been a familiar tree in northern Europe at least since the sixteenth century, but first European contact with the blue Atlas cedar seems to have been as late as 1827. Then, so the story goes, the English botanist Philip Baxter Webb, who co-authored *The Natural History of the Canary Islands*, was shown a specimen branch in Tangiers by an Arab who had brought it down from the mountains.

The Atlas cedar is tall and pyramidal when young, but spreads out in middle age with a broad canopy that can equal, in diameter, more than half its height – in other words it needs plenty of space. The colour of its leaf-needles varies from green through grey-blue to the striking silver-blue (var. *glauca*) that one sees outgrowing so many suburban shrubberies. The colour most commonly seen in the Atlas forests is grey-blue, produced by a waxy deposit that occurs on conifers in drought-affected regions.

The Atlas is the most robust and versatile of the three cedar species. It does not care much whether the ground is acid or alkaline, is indifferent to extremes of frost or heat, and, once its wide-spreading roots are established, will see off the most vicious drought. It is long-lived – up to 500 years. Be careful not to plant one too near your home, though, or

you will be on the telephone to your insurance agent about cracks and subsidence. It is a tidy tree: its needles, unlike those of larches, do not drop off in winter. Little barrel-shaped cones grow upright out of their clusters.

Cedar has a lovely smell and brown colour, is popular with carpenters and builders and resists boring insects. Its greatest predator has always been man. In recent years, during the drought in Morocco, troops of macaque monkeys – otherwise known as Barbary apes – have done great damage to parts of the cedar forests by stripping the trees down to their cadmium layer and chewing the bark for its water content. Other species, like oak, have not been affected. It was found that shepherds, by enclosing springs with concrete as wells for their livestock, were excluding the monkeys, and that the highly territorial monkeys were driven to attacking cedars for a drink. Artificial watering points for the monkeys have proved the answer.

Louis-Hubert Lyautey never succeeded, of course, in his ambition of replanting the Atlas from end to end with blue cedars. But at least he made a start. Today near Azrou, the 4,000-foot-high hill town in the Middle Atlas, where holidaying Moroccans go to escape the heat of Meknes and Fez, you can see and smell his legacy in the wonderful, sweet-smelling Forêt de Cèdres, where old-growth trees grow side by side with the cedars he planted nearly a century ago.

Opposite: The higher you climb, the taller they grow. Members of the Altlas cedar species reach more than 120 feet at higher altitudes.

Taiga Forest of
Northern Russia

'I long for scenes where man hath never trod

A place where woman never smiled or wept

There to exist with my Creator God

And sleep as I in childhood sweetly slept

Untroubling and untroubled where I lie

The grass below, above the vaulted sky'

I am, written in 1848 by John Clare, pastoral poet of England

Page 60: Leaves rest on a carpet of moss in the swampy, coniferous forests of the taiga.

Page 61: Severe weather conditions limit survival to only the hardiest of species.

Opposite: Although recent satellite- and field-study has revealed blocks of old growth, most of the taiga is secondary re-growth.

If, on a clear day in summer, you were to look down on the top of the world through the window of a spaceship, you would see a snow-white Pole surrounded by an indigo Arctic Ocean; and below it, in the far north of European and Asian Russia, from the Baltic Shield across the Urals to the Bering Sea, a broad, unbroken rug of fluffy green wool. This is the Russian taiga, defined in the *Dictionary of the Living Russian Language* (1903) as 'vast, uninterrupted forests, unpassable ancient remoteness, an absence of human dwellings over a great expanse'. The taiga, a huge area of forests, bogs, lakes, rivers, flood meadows, mountain tundra and rocky outcrops, is one of the last great wildernesses on earth.

If, having landed from your spaceship, you were to walk south out of the permafrost tundra, say down the 45-degree longitude line, east of Archangel, you would first encounter a narrow band of birch (which grows beyond the last pine in northern latitudes), then isolated, fairly open stands of Scots pine and Norway spruce (aka Christmas trees) growing along river valleys sticking northwards into the tundra and sheltered from northern winds. Here, in a wilderness of bogs and lakes, winters are bitter-cold, lasting six months or more, with mean temperatures well below freezing, and the summers very short, with only fifty to a hundred frost-free days. The needle-leaves of the conifers are well adapted to these harsh conditions. Their narrowness reduces transpiration (handy when the frozen ground in winter prevents trees from replenishing their water supply). A thick waxy coating over their needles protects them from icy winds and they can shuffle off accumulated snow. And because they are dark and evergreen, they can absorb the heat of the sun and begin photosynthesis as soon as the spring days are warm enough, without having to waste time growing leaves.

Opposite: The slim silver birch grows in the very northernmost areas of the chilly taiga.

As you proceed farther south, the canopy becomes darker, more closed. Spruce, fir, pine and deciduous larch become the dominant species. Here, in an under-storey of birch, aspen, willow and alder, lynxes and various members of the weasel family (wolverine, fisher, pine marten, mink, ermine and sable) stalk their prey: hares and red squirrels, lemmings and voles. Far away to the east, at the Asiatic end of the taiga, the largest wild cats in the world, Amur tigers (very few are left now), hunt wild boars in old-growth forests of Manchurian oak and Korean pine. All over the taiga, reindeer and elk browse the moss, cottongrass and heather at the base of the trees. A reminder of those who hunted the elk (and herded the reindeer) are the frequently encountered ruins of old wooden hunting cabins dating back to Tsarist times.

In those happy, pre-lapsarian days the taiga was, in the jargon of foresters, 'skimmed': the best trees were felled, hauled by horse up to six miles to the nearest river landing and floated downstream. You can still come across mossy, ivy-covered stumps of trees cut down more than a century ago. Then came the Bolshevik Revolution, and with it the egregious S.S. Lobov, People's Commissar for Soviet Forestry in the 1930s. He scorned the, on the whole, sustainable forestry of the 'kulaks' (rich peasants) and chillingly recommended that 'the basic principle of forest utilisation during the second five-year plan must be clearcuts of unrestricted size' (*Two Hundred Years of the Forest Department,* 1998). For 'unrestricted size' read 'landscape size'. The old-growth pines, firs and spruces that once dominated the taiga – both with a seed-range of only about 300 feet – became the target of a murderous assault. A recent satellite- and field-study by Global Forest Watch and Greenpeace Russia has revealed that blocks of intact, old-growth Scots pine and spruce forest (a 'block' being defined as 50,000 hectares plus, with a minimum width of 10 km) account for only about 14 per cent (32 million hectares) of the total forest area of northern European Russia. The rest, to a greater or lesser degree, is secondary re-growth after clear-felling: birch, goat-willow and alder whose readily germinating seeds spread wide on the wind.

Russia has some of the tightest timber laws in the world – and one of the worst records in applying them. The devaluation of the Russian rouble, following the 1998 financial crisis, made it highly profitable to extract timber for export, a fact not lost on Russian timber companies like Primorlesprom, which has blocks of old-growth taiga trees in its sights. In May 2003 President Putin (who is on record as having called the Russian forests an 'ecological shield for the entire planet') transferred environmental responsibility for the taiga away from the environmentally conscious Federal Forest Service into the hands of the Russian Ministry of Natural Resources, which has a track record of aggressive exploitation.

In September 2003, the Kremlin approved a new draft Forest Code allowing long-term concession and privatisation of forests. The draft, it is hoped, will shortly be approved by the Russian parliament. The taiga, one of Europe's and Asia's last great wildernesses, awaits, once again, the chainsaw.

Previous pages: A logger's paradise: the Kremlin has recently reopened the taiga to exploitation.

Next pages: Conifers are well adapted to the harsh conditions of the taiga winter, which can last more than six months.

The Valley of the Giants, Tasmania

Page 72: The Tasmanian devil. Now extinct on the Australian mainland, these marsupials are unique to Tasmania.

Page 73: A rare sight – swamp gum forest.

On the western coast of Tasmania, where rain-heavy winds sweep in along the fortieth parallel from Patagonia, about ninety minutes' drive from the state capital, Hobart, there is an old-growth forest that contains small, isolated groves of huge, emergent trees. Until a few years ago, the forest, lying just outside the Franklin National Park, was more or less unknown, visited only by the odd backpacker, an infrequent fisherman, or a logger eyeing new supplies.

The valley of the River Styx, which divides the Snowy and Maydena mountain ranges, is one of the last remaining habitats on Earth of the so-called swamp gum (*Eucalyptus regnans*), which holds all kinds of records: Australia's tallest eucalypt, the world's tallest flowering plant, the world's tallest hardwood tree, the southern hemisphere's tallest tree, perhaps even, when the last, biggest *regnans* has been felled and measured, the world's tallest tree.

Above: The swamp gum can reach up to 22 feet in girth. As older, bigger trees are felled, younger rivals do not have to compete for position in the forest canopy. As a result they are growing less tall.

At the beginning of the nineteenth century, when British settlers from New South Wales sailed across the Bass Strait to colonise Tasmania, *regnans* was fairly common throughout the island. Now, only about 13 per cent of the original old-growth trees remain. Their scarcity makes it difficult to understand why, even as I write, some of these marvellous old giants are still being cut down for woodchips. Five hundred years of growth destroyed by a chainsaw in fifteen minutes. Down to the ocean on a lorry, chipped into a huge heap on the dockside, away in a ship's hold to Japan, and back again as newsprint for the tabloids.

Left: Until a few years ago, the Tasmanian forest was more or less unknown and unvisited; today it sits in the crosshairs of logging companies.

Australia is home to about six hundred species of eucalypts (members of the Myrtle family), which range in size from mallee bushes (from whose severed roots desert-travelling aborigines extract drinking water) to tall rainforest trees. The leaves of eucalypts tend to be narrow, leathery and scimitar-shaped, like willow leaves, and they generally hang down from the branches on which they grow. This helps to prevent overheating in the fierce Australian sunshine, and in the forests allows light to penetrate their high canopy, encouraging a luxuriant growth of ferns and shrubs (in the case of *regnans*, olearia and acacia) on the forest floor below. The bark of most eucalypts is deciduous; that is, it flakes off in strips every season, revealing eye-catching patterns of greys and greens, or even pink. *Regnans* is known, in the vernacular, as Swamp Gum because it likes undrained ground and high rainfall, and will grow well beside water. The upper half of its trunk tends to have smooth, deciduous bark; the bark of its lower half is persistent and hairy. In the Tasmanian summer its canopy blooms with a show of rather nondescript, small white flowers. It is not very hardy. If its top is frosted it dies.

It is the sheer size of *Eucalyptyus regnans* that is so astonishing. You could park several cars across the base of a big one. If you stand beside one and look up, it is like craning your neck to peer up the side of a skyscraper. The average height of a *regnans* forest canopy is 195 to 230 feet, but the big ones regularly grow to 270 feet and more. The tallest recorded so far in the Styx valley reached 302 feet, and there may be other, bigger specimens: up to 330 feet, some say, the length of a football field, in competition for the world tree record, currently held by a Californian redwood, of 368 feet.

For millennia, the forest floor of the Styx valley has been home to wallabies, bandicoots, pygmy possums and Tasmanian devils (bear-like marsupials with a characteristic, low, yelling growl followed by a snarling cough). Tasmanian devils may be disagreeable on first acquaintance, but they are no threat to humans. Tasmanian wolves, with tiger-like stripes – the last sighting in the wild was in 1936 – used to roam these parts. Up above in the canopy you have a fair chance of seeing a wedge-tailed eagle (Australia's largest bird of prey, and on the endangered list) or a white goshawk.

Over the past four years a war has been waged between the state government and logging companies, who wish to clear-fell the Styx valley forest and replace it with plantations, and environmentalists who want the Australian federal government to declare the valley a National Park, with World Heritage status. In 1999 the Wilderness Society of Australia dressed up one of the biggest trees with 3,000 Christmas lights – the job took a team of climbers eight days – to publicise their conservation efforts. The Tasmanian logging industry, which is worth $1.3 billion a year and employs 10,000 people, argues that *regnans* is fully protected in the Franklin National Park to the north; that 40 per cent of the island's land area and forests are already protected in reserves; and that any trees in the Styx over 265 feet will be spared. The environmentalists object, saying that firebombing and chemical poisoning of re-growth by loggers is indiscriminate and lethal to wildlife. They have drawn attention to one 265-foot giant whose roots were exposed by a bulldozer and whose trunk had been cooked and killed, from inside to out, by a logger's forest fire. In the mythology of the Ancient Greeks, the River Styx wound seven times around the Land of the Dead. Today, if Tasmania's Styx valley remains unprotected, it threatens to turn the old myth into a grotesque modern reality: an underworld of dead trees.

Opposite: The giant Australian and Tasmanian tree fern (*Dicksonia antarctica*) is common throughout the Styx forests.

Californian Kelp Forest

One might have thought that, if there was one part of our planet reasonably safe from human degradation, it would be the great underwater forests of seaweed that prosper around our cooler coasts. One would be wrong. By the 1950s it was becoming obvious that one of the world's largest and most species-rich kelp forests, which grows off the coast of central California, was fast disappearing. One reason was readily apparent: the number of sea otters in the area (which feed on the sea urchins that graze on kelp seedlings) had dwindled. They were not eating enough sea urchins to give the kelp a chance.

Opposite and previous pages: The canopy of the kelp forest is buoyed up by gas bladders, which keep photosynthesising fronds at the surface.

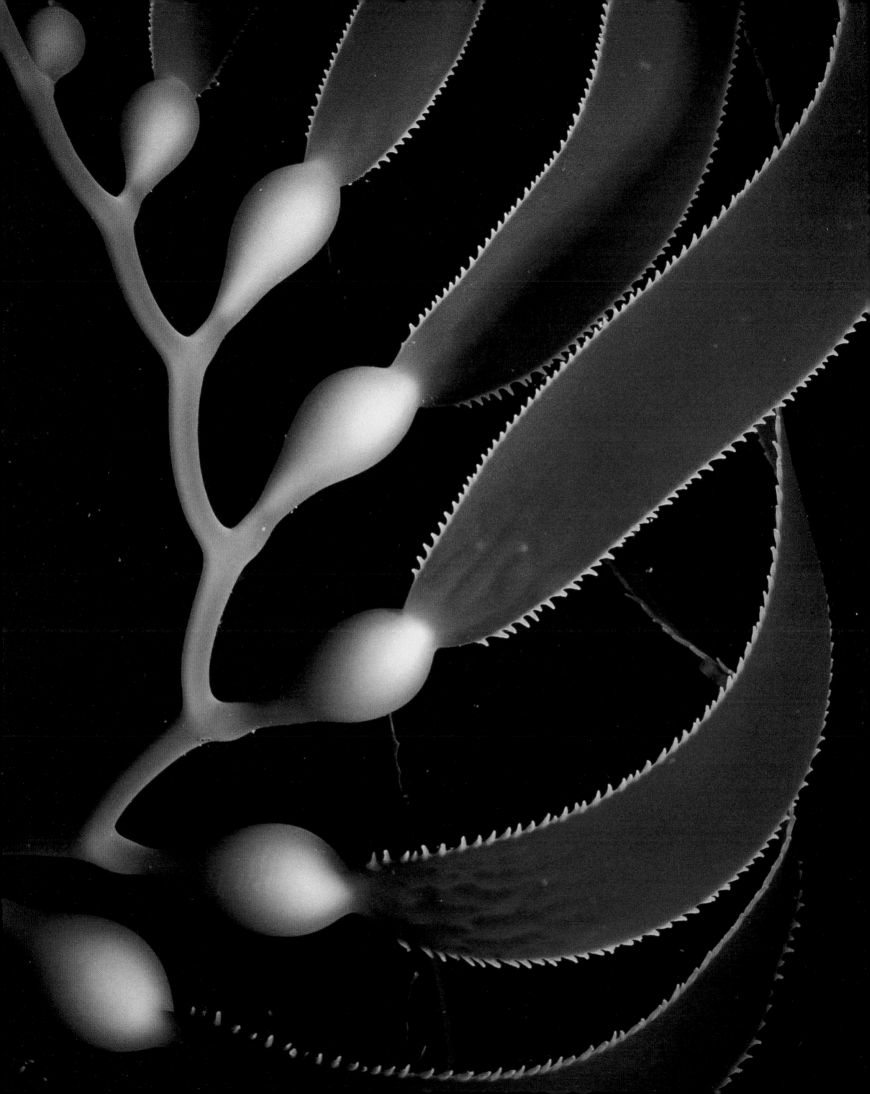

Giant kelp (*Macrocystis pyrifera*) grows throughout the world in shallow, open coastal waters where temperatures do not rise above about 20°C (68°F). It thrives all down the west coast of North America, from Alaska to Mexico, and nowhere more than off California, where it can grow at the astonishing rate of over two feet a day. Its favourite habitats are rocky reefs in 6 to 100 feet of water.

Although it resembles a plant, giant kelp lacks a vascular system – it is in fact a perennial alga with a life expectancy of about seven years. Seedling kelps attach themselves to reefs by root-like structures called 'holdfasts', and reach up towards the surface and the light with long stems called 'stipes', which can extend for 100 feet or more. At the surface they form a dense and spreading canopy of photosynthesising fronds, which are buoyed up by gas-bladders – we all remember as children the slimy sensation of popping the bladders under our bare feet along the top of the tide. The holdfasts need to be strong enough to withstand, and even slow down, the to-and-fro surges of wave and tide. Sometimes, particularly in winter storms, they give way and huge rafts of kelp float off into the open ocean and continue to grow on the surface until they encounter warmer water or are beached. For early sailors, drifting kelp meant land was near.

The Monterey Bay National Marine Sanctuary, south of San Francisco, runs 276 miles along the shore and, on average, 30 miles out into the ocean. It was established by the US Federal government in 1992 to protect one of these wonderful kelp forests, the nation's largest.

Opposite: The most spectacular algae on Earth: giant Californian kelp reaches the water's surface.

The kelp-cutting barges that, in summer, once chugged up and down in the lee of the Santa Lucia hills, slicing off the top of the canopy (so that alginate thickeners for the food-processing industry could be extracted from its slick mucus) frightened off the shy, urchin-eating otters, who departed in despair. Today, all kelp harvesting is banned in the sanctuary

from April to July, joining a list of other full-time don'ts that include oil and gas drilling, disposing of industrial waste, discharging effluent, dredging, low-flying planes and motor-boating, outside authorised routes. The ocean is cleaner and quieter. The otters are coming back. So is the kelp.

Above: A teeming underwater wildlife habitat. Some residents hide in the leafy canopy floating at the surface, or drift among the swaying strands below. Others prefer the rocky bottom, where the giant kelp is anchored to the ocean floor.

Kelp forests, just like terrestrial forests, support very delicate ecosystems, all too easily upset. They provide hiding places for prey and predator alike. Down on the ocean floor, among the holdfasts, live sea urchins, sponges, crustaceans, starfish and sea anemones. Below the canopy, through a tangled water column of kelp stipes and algal fronds, nose harbour seals and sea otters, bottlenose dolphins and sea lions, turtles and porpoises, even whales. In all, the sanctuary is home to five hundred species of marine mammals, seabirds, fish, turtles and invertebrates; not to mention around four hundred and fifty species of large marine algae.

The best way to see the Monterey kelp forest and its denizens is to scuba dive down into it. Wet suits are necessary, for water temperatures are fairly cool, averaging 13°C (55°F) year-round, with visibility varying from 20 to 30 feet and at its clearest in late autumn. One is advised to make sure that one's equipment is well streamlined, with tabs taped on the inside to avoid getting tangled in the kelp, and to descend feet first, making two slow 360-degree turns on the surface to push the kelp away (the same when coming up). The aim is to cause as little disturbance as possible to this remarkable and fragile environment, while enjoying its wonders. Even turning over an innocent-looking stone can have a deleterious effect.

The Monterey Bay Marine Sanctuary, which was established more than a decade ago, is an illustration of what can be achieved when enough determination, money and enforcement are forthcoming: a fabulous, diverse, self-regenerating submarine forest to delight our own and future generations.

Mediterranean Maquis and Garigue

In California they call it *chaparral*; in Chile *matorral*; in Spain *tomillares*; in Italy *macchia*; in Australia *mallee*; in South Africa *fynbos* or *veld*. And in France they call it *maquis*. Its summer, the dormant period, is very dry and hot, with long droughts; its growing time, winter, is short and rainy. Its vegetation, adapted to the dry conditions, is a dense, mostly impenetrable tangle of woody shrubs with names like thorny broom, myrtle, lentisc, box, buckthorn and the turpentine tree, which grows to between 6 and 16 feet high, with small, broad, evergreen, stiff, thick, hard-skinned leaves. Beneath the shrubs, in open glades, grow aromatic and herbaceous herbs, both annual and perennial; above them, providing a little shade, an open, sparse canopy of small trees – evergreen oak, cork, sweet chestnut, against whose trunks shepherds, goatherds and readers and writers of pastoral poetry have reclined after a good lunch, and fallen asleep.

Page 92: Roccapina, Corsica.

Page 93: Font Roja, one of the best preserved native Mediterranean forests in Spain. That this forested enclave survived is chiefly thanks to the difficult terrain which hindered its exploitation. The area is home to populations of wild boar, weasel, fox, and badger.

Opposite: In spring, the *garigue* erupts in a profusion of irises, crocuses, jonquils, orchids and violets.

Ten thousand years ago, before historic times, dense forests of oak and pine grew more or less right around the shores of the Mediterranean and throughout its islands, in the so-called olive belt, with gaps, of course, along the south-western littoral past Egypt. Then came the Bronze and Iron Ages, with their axes, charcoal-burners, farmers and home-builders – and, worst of all, hungry herds of goats, both feral and domestic, which gobbled up the oak and pine seedlings required for forest renewal. By Greek and Roman times huge parts of the Mediterranean world – all of Sicily, for example – had become bare of trees. Fertile river valleys were entirely farmed; hillsides not terraced for olive, vine, apricot, almond or fig were abandoned to secondary scrub growth (in other words, *maquis*). Only the most inaccessible places, like gorges and cliff faces, remained intact.

If the *maquis* is further degraded by repeated forest fires or extreme over-grazing, especially on chalky soils, it becomes what the French call *garigue*, consisting of scattered dwarf bushes, mostly less than 20 inches high, with bare patches of rock, sand or stony ground in between. A further downgrade and it turns into *lande* or steppe: a wasteland of mostly herbaceous plants with the occasional low, woody, rather sad little shrub.

The Mediterranean basin, which represents, in terms of land area, only about 1.5 per cent of the Earth's surface, may have lost much of its forest, but more than a hundred tree species still survive in the wild there, as compared to about thirty in central Europe. More than one in ten plants, for example, of the larger islands like Corsica, Crete and Sicily do not exist elsewhere, and the region contains nine endemic species of fir tree, some of them found only in remote niches in the mountains: *Abies pinsapo* in southern Spain, *Abies numidica* in the Babor mountains of Algeria, *Abies nebrodensis* in Sicily.

Who can ever forget the hot, languorous smell of the *maquis*, from the path that winds its way down through the umbrella stone pines to the shore of a crystalline sea? The scents of rosemary and myrtle, juniper and cistus, lavender and thyme linger, like wood smoke, in the memory. Or who could remain blind, in spring, to the beauty of the *garigue*, when it erupts with irises and crocuses, jonquils and narcissi, orchids and helleborines, anemones and violets? In spring the *garigue*, and in summer the *maquis*, seem a paradise, a paradigm of an older and wiser world. For all their beauty, though, it is worth remembering that both are the products of human deforestation. They are an ancient warning of the ease with which forests are lost and of the difficulties involved in restoring them.

Next pages: Only the most inaccessible places – gorges and high cliff faces – have provided shelter for the few trees remaining along the shores of the Mediterranean.

The Petrified Forest
of Arizona

Previous pages:
Some trunk segements
of *Araucarioxylon*
represent giant trees
estimated to have been
up to 200 feet high.

On the high, desert plateau of north-eastern Arizona, about a hundred miles south-east of the Grand Canyon and the Colorado river, there exists a world where time seems to have stopped: the so-called Chinle Formation, otherwise known as Arizona's Petrified Forest National Park. Here, long before human history began, and many millions of years before the Spanish explorer Francisco

de Coronado first stumbled through these parts in 1540, a great tropical forest once grew. Its primitive remains now provide us with the largest and best-preserved collection of wood fossils anywhere in the world – a storehouse of knowledge about life on Earth in the Late Triassic period between 200 and 250 million years ago, at the beginning of the Age of the Dinosaurs.

Above: The first fossils were discovered and mythologised by Native American peoples. The Piutes believed the petrified fragments were spent arrow shafts sent by their thunder god, Shinauav. Other tribes built dwellings out of the logs.

Right: The western
diamondback rattlesnake.
One of the largest
species of rattlesnake in
the world, and one of the
most dangerous, is
common to the Petrified
Forest National Park.

At that time, when the world was still a single land mass, Pangea, this part of Arizona was not a high desert plateau but a low, humid equatorial floodplain: something like the basin of the Congo or the Amazon, but with a very different botany. This, after all, was at least 100 million years before the angiosperms, the flowering plants, set out to colonise the planet from what is now Central Africa, and the trees here, at that time, would have been coniferous pines, some of them 9 feet in diameter, and up to 200 feet high. A thick-growing under-storey of ferns, cycads (halfway between pines and palms) and horsetails, in the swamps and along the numerous rivers and streams, would have been home to a diversity of insects, many now extinct, and to reptiles. Giant fish-eating amphibians, outsize armadillos and small primitive dinosaurs would have blinked their prehistoric eyes amid the foliage.

Most of the fossilised logs that now litter the desert landscape with their rainbow colours derive from a single species of pine, long since extinct, called *Araucarioxylon arizonicum*; two others, *Woodworthia* and *Schilderia*, also extinct, occur in small numbers in the northern end of the 93,500-acre park. Uprooted by wind, earthquake or flood, living trees would have been carried by rivers into the floodplains and left high and dry when the waters receded. Most of them decomposed and disappeared. A few, covered in a mixture of silt and silicate ash blown in on the wind from adjacent volcanoes, would have turned into fossils and become part of the Chinle Formation, itself deeply buried by the strata of succeeding millennia. About 60 million years ago, continental convulsions lifted the floodplains to their present eminence as part of the high Colorado plateau, and time and erosion exposed Chinle's secrets. Now the logs of its fossilised trees can be seen lying strewn across clay hills or emerging from the sides of bluffs. It is as if some prehistoric logger has cut the trees with a chainsaw and left the cords just as they fell. Petrified logs, made of quartz, are hard and brittle and snap easily under stress. It wasn't a human hand, but the ancient convulsion of the land, in its progress from floodplain to plateau, that was responsible for the breaking-up.

The land is arid, desolate, wind-blown, undulating, rather nondescript: grey gravel and bleak boulder. In summer, daytime temperatures can soar into the hundreds, and nothing much grows here except sagebrush and patches of prairie grass. But what transfixes the eye are the fossilised logs and their extraordinary rainbow colours, as if some demented artist has been let loose with pots of paint. The colours have in fact been created by an aeon-slow process of petrification. Ground water first dissolved silica from an overlay of silt and volcanic ash, then carried it in solution through the buried logs, where the silica crystallised as quartz and slowly replicated, cell by cell, the original structure of the wood. Iron-rich minerals combined with the quartz to produce the brilliant colours we see today: hematite for red and pink; hydrated iron oxide for yellow, brown and orange; pure iron for green; pure silica for white.

With a permit, you can backpack into the park for overnight camping, or just cruise through it in a car. If you are lucky, you may catch a glimpse of a desert cottontail (a small rabbit), a tiny kangaroo rat (which gets all the water it needs from eating seeds), a black-tailed jackrabbit (a hare) or even a herd of pronghorn (antelope-like, and the-fastest-over-a-short-burst animal in North America). Be warned, though: this is rattlesnake country, and rabbits and prairie dogs may be infected with plague or, worse, rabies. Park literature rather quaintly enjoins you to respect rattlesnakes' 'personal space'. Whatever you do, though, leave the fossilised logs or fragments where they lie. It is estimated that tourists illegally remove about a ton of wood fossils from the park every month. The Petrified Forest has lasted for 200 million years. Let it lie a little longer undisturbed.

Opposite: Daytime temperatures in the Petrified Forest regularly soar into the hundreds; nothing much grows here except sagebrush and prairie grass.

Next pages: Over a long period, water containing dissolved minerals seeped into the wood and replaced the organic cells with stone. Much later, the whole area was uplifted and eroded to shape the present landscape.

Sherwood Forest

It is a pleasant irony. Sherwood, one of the most legendary forests in the world, was never, in medieval times, continuous woodland; rather, it was a sandy-soiled heathland growing heather, bracken and gorse, interspersed with about fifteen discrete stands of oak and birch, none of them much bigger than a few hundred acres. The heath itself was vast, extending from Nottingham north to Worksop; 20 miles long, and between 5 and 9 miles broad: plenty of room for an outlaw to hide in, especially in summer, but not necessarily up the nearest tree.

Previous pages: Gnarled oak and fungus.
Right: Sherwood Forest, made famous by the
legend of Robin Hood, is home to some of the
oldest trees in England.

The misnomer is all the Conqueror's fault. He and his Normans brought over with them the notion of a forest – the word never existed in Anglo-Saxon England – as a sporting and larder area, where the game belonged to the king. It often implied a much greater acreage than the woods where the deer and boar lay up, and the phrase persists today in the Scottish Highlands, where deer forests are open moorland, not woods. The royal forests – twenty-five are mentioned in 1086 in the Domesday Book (where the word first occurs) – were resented by Englishmen, high and low. They conferred a royal right to roam and hunt, and Magna Carta put a stop to their increase in 1215. Landowners and common-graziers alike resented the Forest Laws, with their attendant officials, fines, and not-inconsiderable demands from the king. When Henry III sat down for his Christmas dinner in 1251, his various forests, from Carlisle to Kent, had been obliged to provide 430 red deer, 200 each of fallow deer, roe deer, wild swine (specifically from the Forest of Dean, the last remaining source), 1,300 hares, 4,500 rabbits, 2,100 partridges, 290 pheasants, 395 swans, 115 cranes, 80 salmon and numerous lampreys.

Opposite: Frost-covered bracken (*Pteridium aquilinum*).

Previous pages: Early
morning mist in a stand
of young growth and
bracken.

William's fourth and youngest son, Henry I of England – he who said that an unlettered king is only a crowned ass – was probably responsible for declaring Sherwood a royal forest; it gets its first mention as such in 1154, nineteen years after his death, the year his grandson, Henry II, came to the throne. In 1215, when John was king, the *Sherwood Forest Book* detailed how the heathland should be managed and listed fifteen woods and groves, including Birkland (Birkelonde), which still stands today. The earliest-known map of the forest, dating from 1774, shows a huge tract of heath (65,000 acres) and smaller areas of defined woodland. Included on the 1774 map are the woods and great parks of the 'Dukeries': Welbeck, Clumber, Thoresby, Rufford, Clipstone and Newstead Abbey. It was at Newstead that Lord Byron toasted his friends from a human skull.

If you are determined to imagine Robin Hood and Will Scarlett lying, like leopards, along the branch of an ancient oak, on the lookout for a fat abbot and his purse (rather than lying-up in roadside bracken, which footpads of that period are thought to have favoured), the best place to visit is the Hay of Birklands, a 450-acre area of medieval oak-and-birch woodland near the village of Edwindstowe and now a country park run by Nottinghamshire County Council. Here, only a short walk from café, souvenir shop and car park, you can imagine yourself back into the Middle Ages and beyond. Growing out of the bracken around you are stands of several hundred huge oaks that date back more than five hundred years. They look their age, gesticulating with dead, pointed branches against the grey Nottingham sky; each, as Shakespeare put it, with its 'high top bald with dry antiquity'. Here, according to legend, once grew Robin Hood's Larder, a hollow oak, where he is said to have hung his poached venison. One veteran that has survived is the Major Oak, now fenced off to stop visitors compacting the ground and denying it moisture. It has a short, thick trunk and a circumference of 33 feet, and is thought to be between 800 and 1,000 years old. Its branches and foliage, despite an old man's props and hawsers, seem in good fettle.

And what of Robin? Did he exist? The closest historians have come to hard evidence about him is a document of 1226: the Sheriff of Yorkshire owed thirty-two shillings and six pence in the matter of the chattels of Robert Hood, fugitive. The best guess is that Robin was a thirteenth-century outlaw from Barnsdale, west Yorkshire, some thirty miles north of Sherwood, and that most of his exploits took place in the Barnsdale area. This is a disappointment to those who believe in his legend, but in the end, it does not matter much, even if he has to be a Yorkshireman. Like Sherwood Forest, he exists, and will continue to exist, in the English imagination.

Left: The Major Oak. Its enormous hollow interior is a home for hibernating insects and mammals such as bats, queen wasps, butterflies and a variety of spiders.

The Kauri Pine Forests of New Zealand

Whenever standards of excellence are quoted for timber, teak from Burma, mahogany from Cuba, hickory from North America and kauri pine from New Zealand are names that top any list. Kauri pine is remarkable for its strength, durability, and for the ease with which it is worked. In the old days of sail and square-riggers, immature stands of kauri, known as 'rickers', were felled in thousands for masts and spars. It is a tragedy that its excellence as timber has been its undoing.

Previous pages and opposite: Many trees in the kauri lived undisturbed for 2,000 years, until the nineteenth century brought loggers to New Zealand.

The coniferous kauri pine, *Agathis australis,* is a native of New Zealand's North Island, the only place in the world it grows. It ranges from the North Cape down past Auckland to about 38 degrees south, a region where warm westerlies blow in across the Tasman Sea from southern Australia. The landscape here is low-lying and gently undulating, and the climate mild, with little frost or snow. There are no high mountains. It is ideal for the kauri, which likes a coastal, warm-temperate, sub-tropical environment.

In the latter half of the eighteenth century, when Captain Cook charted New Zealand's coastline and brought the islands within the British ambit, kauri grew abundantly in the North Island forests. Native Maoris made canoes from its timber, tapped the trunks for its resinous gum and hunted pigeons and parrots in its canopy. Most trees lived undisturbed to a ripe old age, some for an astonishing two thousand years. Then, in the nineteenth century, across the Tasman Sea, came waves of European settlers hungry for land. They logged, burned, cleared and degraded the once-great kauri forests so that only about 300 square miles out of the estimated 4,500 square miles that once covered the Northland still remain.

In areas where Kauris allow sun to penetrate the undegrowth, tree ferns and nikau palms – New Zealand's only native palm – carpet the forest floor.

So-called kauri forests are not exclusively kauri – mature pines tend to grow, either on their own or in groups, among smaller broadleaf hardwoods and podocarps (a yew-related, evergreen genus of trees). But the big ones are easy to spot, for they soar above the surrounding canopy like the giant emergents of a Brazilian rainforest. The tallest trees grow to 165 feet, with girths of 50 feet. As they grow, they shed their lower branches, and their huge ash-grey trunks rise straight and clean for 100 feet from the forest floor, with little or no taper. It's obvious why their timber was so prized by loggers.

The best place to see old-growth kauris is on the west coast not far from Auckland, where a stretch of 22,500 acres is protected in the Waipoua Forest Sanctuary. The main road through the sanctuary takes you to within a ten-minute walk of 'Te Matua Ngahere', 'The Father of the Forest'. Its massive trunk is 16 feet in diameter. Close by are the 'Four Sisters', a graceful grove of four tall trees growing hard by one another. A little farther on, and close to the road, stands the magnificent 'Tane Mahuta', 'Lord of the Forest': 1,200 years old, 170 feet high and the tallest and bulkiest kauri in New Zealand. A typical acre of old-growth kauri forest might contain perhaps forty tall, adult trees.

Kauri leaves are stalkless and olive-green and persist for several seasons without falling off. They are thick and leathery, about the size and shape of a bantam's egg, and they form a dense and massive flat-topped or fan-shaped crown, which can be up to 100 feet in diameter and which is supported by thick, upswept branches. Where kauris grow close together, they block any sun from reaching the forest floor, which tends to be bare, covered in a yard-thick humus layer of peeled bark.In more open stands, however, where light can penetrate the canopy, tree ferns, nikau palms and swags of lianas and epiphytes are able to form a second tier, and below them kauri grass, filmy ferns, mosses, liverworts and orchids luxuriate on the forest floor.

Here in the forest, especially at dusk, you may encounter a brown kiwi bird, national emblem of New Zealand. It is about the size of a large chicken, and is flightless, long-billed and mainly nocturnal. It nests in a hole in the ground and feeds on worms and berries. Several thousand live in the Waipoua reserve and the biggest threats to it are cars, dogs and possums. A much rarer species living up in the canopy is the kokako, a wattlebird with a bright-blue fleshy wattle, black beak and grey feathers. Only about a hundred survive at Waipoua. Other forest exotics include the red-crowned parakeet, two species of parrot, a giant grasshopper-like insect called a weta and the kauri snail (which eats earthworms for breakfast and has a large, green-black glossy shell).

All mature kauris in New Zealand, even those on private land, are protected now. Only on very rare occasions is permission granted for a big one to be cut down: for example, to make a ceremonial Maori canoe. Contemporary New Zealanders are justly proud of their magnificent kauris, and they are aware of their long-term potential to draw tourists. Those kauri forests that have survived the clear-cutting of the last two hundred years are now out of danger.

Opposite: Kauri is now protected and cannot be milled for any reason. Because of its beautiful sheen, which appears to change colour with the light, it was a prized material for furniture and crafts.

Baobab Woods of Madagascar

There is an old African legend about baobabs. God grew them first in the Congo basin, but the trees grumbled that the tropical rain made their trunks swell. He moved them to the Mountains of the Moon in East Africa, to the high slopes of the Ruwenzori range. That didn't suit them either: they complained of fogs and damps. To teach them a lesson He pulled up their swollen trunks and threw them into the desert, where they landed upside down with their roots in the air.

Previous pages: A baobab flower and the famous Avenue of the Baobabs in Morondava, Madagascar.

Right: Baobabs in Madagascar – home to six of the eight species of baobab.

God had a good throwing-arm. Of the eight species in the *Adansonia* (baobab) genus, one (*digitata*) landed all over Africa; six stuck in the ground on the drier, west side of Madagascar; and one, with multiple trunks (*gibbosa*), became impaled in the dry creek beds and rocky outcrops of north-western Australia.

The baobabs of Africa and Australia tend to grow on their own, in splendid isolation. But in Madagascar there are enough of them clumped together as a dominant species to form the weirdest of woods. If you hire a bush taxi from the town of Morondava (about two-thirds of the way down the island on the west side) and bump north over a gravel track for twelve miles, you will come through derelict rice paddy fields, worked intermittently by local farmers, to the so-called Avenue of the Baobabs. It is an extraordinary sight: a cluster, either side of the road and beside a large lily pond, of what look like massive classical columns with vegetation sprouting from their tops. The columns are *Adansonia grandidieri* (Grandidier's baobab), the most stately – and most exploited – of all the Malagasy baobabs, and still fairly common all down the west coast.

Grandidier's is the island's largest baobab species, up to 80 feet high. Its huge cylindrical trunk, 10 feet or more across, acts as a water reservoir for the tree during the dry season, from April to October. The wood is soft and light (it belongs to the same family as balsa, the Bombacaceae) and is easily hollowed out. Local people strip its reddish-grey bark from the lower trunks of the more accessible trees and weave the fibres into ropes, baskets, hats and even clothes. One would expect the trees to die, but they thrive: some are reliably dated at more than a thousand years old. Hollowing out their trunks from the bottom up does not upset them either: living trees have been eviscerated to make houses or burial chambers or bus shelters – or even in one case, God help us, a cocktail bar.

The branches of Grandidier's baobab form a twisted, flattened canopy at the top of the tree, and at sunset (the best time to visit the Avenue of the Baobabs) they can be seen gesticulating like madmen against the dying light. They carry leaves during the wet season only and local people like to pick and cook them like spinach. Their large white flowers, which carry nectar for only one night, are pollinated by lemurs (which abound in Madagascar), and the large, woody fruits contain a pleasant, cool-tasting mucilaginous pulp in which the seeds are buried. The fruits often live on the trees into the next dry season, and locals make holes in the trunks to shin up to the high canopy and bring them down like coconuts. They eat the pulp fresh and crush the seeds for cooking oil.

More adventurous baobab-spotters can look for *rubrostipa* in the deciduous forests or dry, 'spiny' scrub-woodland, where it is often the dominant species, along the western and southern coasts. It is smaller than *grandidieri*, and claret-bottle-shaped, with a tight constriction at the top of the trunk just below its reddish-brown branches. At the north end of the island grow two very rare species: *perrieri*, identified by science in 1960 and with only a few individuals at five known sites; and *suarensis*, otherwise known as 'bozy', with an elongated fruit and an equally uncertain future. Its bark is greyish-brown and smooth. Two other hard-to-differentiate species are more common: *madagascariensis*, which grows within yards of the sea on the northwest coast, and *za*, widespread in the west. They tend to have cylindrical trunks with irregular swellings.

Throughout Mozambique the baobab is regarded as taboo, a dwelling place for ancestral spirits who will come and haunt you if you cut one down. You sometimes see corn, or money, or rum-filled giant snail shells laid at a baobab's foot as votive offerings. Superstition has helped the baobabs to survive. But botanists worry that even in places like the Avenue of the Baobabs seedling replacements (the seeds germinate as readily as beans) seldom escape the attentions of browsing sheep and goats. On the wet east coast of the island much of the unique rainforest has already been lost to secondary pasture, degraded by cut-and-burn land-clearance and the pressures of a growing population. This is a pity. Madagascar may be a poor country, but it is also one of the world's great hot-spots of biodiversity. It boasts 8,000 unique plant species (orchids in particular), two-thirds of the world's chameleons, thirty endemic species of lemur, including the golden bamboo lemur discovered only in 1987, an army of reptiles and amphibians, swarms of insects, among them Wallace's hawk-moth, with its 14-inch-long tongue for sucking nectar from, and fertilising, the comet orchid – and of course six unique species of baobab. It is for the time being anyway a naturalist's Promised Land.

Canada's Great Bear Rainforest

The Kitasoo Indians of Canada's west coast tell a Creation myth about Raven, the Great Bird. Raven turned every tenth black bear white to warn and remind the world of its Ice Age past. About four hundred of these white bears still exist. The Indians call them Spirit Bears; taxonomists, more prosaically, call them *Ursus americanus kermodii*, the Kermode Bear. They are in fact a sub-species of the American Black Bear and the only place in the world you can find them is in the Great Bear Rainforest of British Columbia.

The temperate rainforests of the Pacific coast once stretched all the way from Northern California to Alaska. Today, most of the American old-growth trees have gone, clear-felled by logging. Mainly because of its remoteness and inaccessibility, the Great Bear Rainforest of British Columbia has survived and it represents one of the world's rarest, and most endangered, ecosystems. There are other temperate rainforests in the world – in Chile, Tasmania, New Zealand – but the Great Bear is the largest, longest and most continuous.

Previous pages: Douglas fir plantation on Canada's Pacific coast.

Opposite: The Spirit Bear's habitat includes large groves of sitka spruce trees over 800 years old. As old-growth trees on valley slopes are felled, erosion and landslides may block vital salmon streams – one of the the bear's prime food resources.

A forest is defined as a rainforest when it receives more than 80 inches of rain evenly distributed throughout the year. The Great Bear, where it hardly ever stops raining, easily qualifies. Extending along the Pacific shoreline from Knight Inlet (opposite the top end of Vancouver Island) for 310 miles north to the Alaskan Panhandle, it covers an area about the size of Switzerland, 17 million acres of wild and rugged coastline: snow-capped mountains, glaciers, lakes, mighty rivers and waterfalls, steep-sided fjords, mist-shrouded islands separated by whirlpools and tidal rips – and an endless, evergreen rug of pine trees growing out of fog-soaked moss.

This is ideal pine-growing country, acid and wet, and the Great Bear's old-growth trees are awesomely huge, to the envy of foresters worldwide. Douglas firs (*Pseudotsuga menziesii*) have brown, deeply fissured bark and rise, straight as an arrow, for up to 300 feet, with a lifespan of five hundred years or more. Loggers like them because their enormous trunks have only a gradual taper, and the big ones are bare of side branches, and therefore knotless, for about the first 100 feet. Sitka spruce (*Picea sitchensis*), the North American Christmas tree, grows equally tall, in dense stands right down to the water's edge. It gets its name from Sitka, which was the old Russian administrative capital of Alaska on Baranof Island before the territory was ceded to the United States in 1867.

Another dominant tree of the Great Bear is the western red cedar (*Thuja plicata*). With a graceful conical form and smelling strongly of turpentine, at up to 200 feet it is not as tall as the Douglas fir – nor is it, strictly speaking, a true cedar. But its aromatic wood still makes it a highly prized target for the loggers' chainsaws.

If you were to walk in the forest, you would be struck by the way the great trees seem to grow in random straight lines, as if planted along a string. This happens when an old-growth giant falls across the forest floor, and its decaying, moss-covered trunk becomes an ideal raised nursery bed for seedling trees in an otherwise dense undergrowth of ferns and heathery shrubs called salal bushes.

In summer and autumn, the rivers of the Great Bear are full of salmon – coho, sockeye, pink, chum and steelhead – on their annual journey upstream from the sea to the gravel spawning-redds, where they will mate and die. This is banquet time for the bears, wolves and eagles that live in the forest. In the Great Bear, clear-felling the trees (which slow down and filter the flash floods that can silt up, or scour away, the spawning-redds) endangers not just the salmon, and the bears' autumn diet of them, but a whole tranche of life: black-tailed deer, elk, bushy-tailed wood rats, martens, bats, giant salamanders, northern flying squirrels, moss-eating wild goats, all of whom depend on the forest in one way or another. The rare marbled murrelet, now on British Columbia Wildlife Department's 'red' or 'threatened' list, spends most of its life at sea and only returns to the high tops of the Great Bear's pine trees to mate and nest.

Sadly, even in this remarkable old rainforest, the sound of revving chainsaws is never far away – and they are not just cutting up winter firewood either. In April 2001 an agreement was reached between the British Columbian state government, environmental groups, logging companies and so-called 'First Nations' (indigenous Indian tribes), granting protection to twenty intact rainforest valleys in the Great Bear, and temporarily banning industrial logging in sixty-eight others. So far, so good, but two years later, according to Canadian environmentalists, the government is still dragging its feet. The status of nearly every area originally proposed for protection is still to be negotiated, and clear-cutting continues unabated in many central and northern parts of the Great Bear. In September 2003 Greenpeace activists dumped 150 tree stumps in the entrance to the Quebec City Convention Centre, where the UN-sponsored World Forestry Congress was meeting, to highlight what they still regard as the grotesque mismanagement of Canada's forests in general, and of the Great Bear in particular, by the federal and provincial governments.

Not long ago a white Spirit Bear, called Gimpy because he was lame in one of his paws, made friends with the residents of Terrace, a Canadian town up near the Alaskan border. Gimpy was much admired and photographed before he died. As long as the 2001 conservation initiatives are not followed through, the survival not only of Gimpy's entire Spirit Bear sub-species but also great swathes of the much-photographed, much-admired Great Bear ecosystem remains in doubt.

Opposite: Fir-cones of monster trees: the massive Douglas fir is North America's most plentiful softwood species, accounting for over one-fifth of the continent's total softwood reserves.

Next pages: The Great Bear covers 17 million acres of rugged coastline – snow-capped mountains, glaciers, steep fjords and old-growth forests.

Ancient Rainforest of the Cape York Peninsula

I love all waste

And solitary places, where we taste

The pleasure of believing what we see

Is boundless, as we wish our souls to be.

P. B. Shelley, Julian and Maddalo, *written at Este, Lombardy, in the autumn of 1818.*

Page 152: The black cassowary, peculiar to its rainforest habitat and now a rare species.

Page 153: The well-defined layers of a Queensland rainforest.

Opposite: The mangrove forests at Newcastle Bay, Cape York. Covering 125 square miles, they are among the most diverse in the world, a home for 35 different species of mangrove tree.

Australia, in the popular imagination, is a land of desert and drought, of red rock and arid eucalypt. But up in the far north-east of the country, on the east side of Queensland's York Peninsula, which separates the Great Barrier Reef from the Gulf of Carpentaria, there is a green, wet region canopied by ancient rainforest and fed by abundant rain: a land of mountain and gorge, of rushing river and waterfall, of lush vegetation growing down to the shore of the Coral Sea.

Here, just north of the town of Coen, between the McIlwraith and Iron Ranges of mountains, is an area of untouched wilderness covering about 2,000 square miles and containing some of the world's most fascinating – and primitive – rainforest; the sort of woodland that the nineteenth-century German explorer and scientist Baron von Humboldt (who gave his name to the Peruvian current and connected the Amazon with the Orinoco) called, in an inspired phrase, 'the ancient hylaea'. In the context of eternity, most tropical rainforests are surprisingly young. The York Peninsula forest is very, very old.

Palaeobotanists now believe that this fabulous refuge contains many of the world's present-day relics of the ancient forest of Gondwana, the southern supercontinent that 400 million years ago included in one landmass, before they drifted apart, Australia, Antarctica, India, Africa and South America. Here, they say, is one of the world's most important evolutionary museums; a Lost World of endemic, primitive, long-isolated plants, marsupials and song-birds that date back to the beginning of time.

The Cape York rainforest extends along the coast for about ninety miles, with lowland, marshy, mangrove areas by the sea linked to higher mountain plateaus by steep, rugged valleys, down which rivers with names like Massey and Rocky, Chester and Nesbit surge during the rains. The annual rainfall is intense, up to 315 inches, and can vary widely over short distances, depending on how the land lies to the prevailing south-easterly winds. Most of it falls between November and April. Tropical cyclones, in season, are common. As you move west into the rain-shadow of the mountains, the jungle quickly deteriorates into a much more typically Australian landscape of arid, eucalypt savannah. But in the heart of the rainforest the canopy is thick, with little light penetration, and, compared to a Brazilian canopy, only medium-high, 100 to 130 feet above the forest floor. Buff alder, silkwood, crowsfoot elm, silky pine and black bean all do well here, and the under-storey is a swagged vine thicket of rattans and woody palm lianas, strangler figs, walking-stick palms and fleshy herbs. All seven of the world's ancient fern families, and twelve of the world's nineteen primitive flowering-plant (angiosperm) families, occur here, including two specific to Queensland.

Higher up, on the slopes of the mountains, it is colder and wetter; a misty, dripping region of water-saturated aerial mosses suspended from wind-blown shrubs and trees.

The rainforest, high and low, is a wondrous habitat for orchids, butterflies, frogs, mammals and birds. To date, sixty-two genera of orchid

have been identified in the McIlwraith range, including the moth and Cooktown orchids and the spectacular *Vanda hindsii* (more often associated with New Guinea). Frogs range in size from the dwarf rocket frog, three-quarters of an inch in length, to the four-inch giant tree frog. Endemic mammals include the Atherton antechinus (a mouse-like marsupial), the green ring-tailed possum, the musky rat-kangaroo and two species of tree kangaroo. Endemic, too, is the golden bower bird,

so-called because it decorates its bower, or nest, with colourful lichens to attract a mate. Beware, though, of the black cassowary, a bird that can stand over five feet high. It may look like a magnificent, oversized, harmless turkey, with its black feathers, blue head and neck and crimson wattle. But it can be very grumpy if its personal space is threatened, and has sharp nails on its inner toes to prove it.

The remoteness of the York Peninsula forest has been its salvation. Farther down the east coast, between Townsville and Cooktown and round Cairns, there are further areas of rainforest, which in the past, although nominally protected by the State of Queensland as state forests or national parks, have been selectively logged and disturbed on a thirty- to forty-year cycle. In 1988 these southern areas, in spite of bitter opposition from within Queensland, were given World Heritage status by the federal government, and all logging was banned. Now the gaze of loggers, dammers, miners, electricity generators, road-builders and cotton- and sugarcane-growers has moved north, in the direction of the York Peninsula forest.

*Left: All seven of the world's ancient fern families thrive in the Cape York rainforest. The most common and most widespread, the scaly tree fern (*Cyathea cooperi*), is also the largest, growing to a height of 10 feet with a trunk 11 inches thick.*

As I write, a concerned Wildneress Society of Australia is running a campaign for their equal elevation to the World Heritage podium. State ownership, the Wilderness Society argues, can provide only moderate protection: big business is as good at evading local restrictions as the orchid poachers of McIlwraith at dodging overstretched and underfunded park wardens. In the end it will come down to extra money, and who pays the bill. That, in a way, is a side issue: mere ways and means. What is at stake is the survival of one of the most extraordinary primitive wildernesses on our planet.

Opposite: Many rainforest trees have buttressed roots which flare out from the trunk, a support in times of flooding.

Forest Fact File

Amazon Rainforest

Area: 2.3 million square miles.

Rainfall: 80 to 400 inches.

Temperature: 22 to 34°C. Humidity: 90%.

Access: By boat up rivers, and into swamp forest during annual floods.

Look out for: Kapok tree (*Ceiba pentandra*) with giant buttressed roots, jaguar, harpy eagle, giant river otter, puma, macaw, guan, curassaw, black caiman, ocelot, tapir, tambaqui, pink freshwater dolphin, *cobra grande.*

Black Wood of Rannoch

Location: South shore of Loch Rannoch, 23 miles west of Pitlochry, Perthshire, Scotland.

Area: about four square miles.

Rainfall: 50 inches.

Temperature: 3°C (January) to 13°C (July).

Access: The Black Wood is owned and conserved by the Forestry Commission, with all-year-round free access and free car parking at the Carie Burn.

Look out for: Old-growth Scots pines (remnants of the ancient Caledonian pine forest that once covered the Highlands), pine marten, wildcat, crossbill, capercaillie, black grouse.

Sundarban Mangrove Forests of the Ganges Delta

Location: Bay of Bengal, 100 miles south-east of Kolkata (Calcutta).

Area: 3,800 square miles of mangroves and water, now a National Park. The Sundarbans Reserve, a core area set up as a UNESCO World Heritage Site to conserve the Royal Bengal tiger, covers 998 square miles adjoining India's border with Bangladesh.

Rainfall: 80 inches.

Temperature: 20°C to 34°C. Humidity high (80%). Monsoon mid-June to mid-September, fine weather December until March. Cyclones can be expected in May and October–November, often accompanied by dangerous tidal waves.

Access: Difficult and rather dangerous. An average 20 tiger attacks on humans (mainly honey- and wood-collectors and fishermen) reported in the reserve each year. Guided tours by motorboat or rowboat (preferable because silent) available from Sajnakhali, 28 miles south east of Port Canning, the nearest railhead. Mangrove Information Centre recently completed at Sajnakhali. Entry to tiger reserve by permit only, guide compulsory.

Look out for: Sundari tree, Bengal tiger, saltwater crocodile, Olive Ridley turtle, Gangetic dolphin, white-bellied sea-eagle, brown-winged kingfisher, wild boar, spotted deer, swamp francolin.

FIG. 53.—CEDRUS ATLANTICA (SEE P. 423.)

Cloud Forests of the Andes

Location: In the cordilleras between about 6,000 and 12,500 feet, from the Caribbean to Argentina and especially in Colombia, Peru and Bolivia.

Area: In discontinuous strips, about 20 miles wide, for about 1,600 miles.

Rainfall: 80 to 400 inches.

Temperature: From near-freezing to tropical, depending on altitude (a fall of about 1.65°C for every 1,000 feet climbed).

Look out for: Orchids, tree-ferns, spectacled bears, tapirs, condors, bearded howler-monkeys.

Blue Cedar Forests of the Atlas

Location: In widely scattered stands in the foothills of the Middle Atlas mountains, especially on the north side.

Area: 500 square miles throughout Morocco – the largest southern Mediterranean forest, and one of the last relics of a cedar forest that once grew right around the Mediterranean. Densest stands are in the Forêt de Cèdres, south of Azrou.

Rainfall: 19 inches.

Temperature: Freezing to 43°C. Average in summer 24°C, average in winter 11°C.

Access: Free, by car or hiking trails.

Look out for: Macaque monkeys, ancient 'Gouraud' cedar in Forêt de Cèdres (General Gouraud was Lyautey's second-in-command).

Taiga Forest of Northern Russia

Location: Eurasian Russia below the Arctic Circle, between the Baltic Shield and the Bering Sea.

Area: About 1.3 million square miles.

Rainfall: 15 to 20 inches, with low evaporation and high humidity.

Temperature: Minus 32° to plus 32°C (both recorded at Verkhoyansk in Siberia).

Access: Difficult (especially because of visas and red tape). Best in February or March, on cross-country skis, when days are lengthening and temperatures rising.

Look out for: Scots pine, Norway spruce, silver birch, lynx, wild boar, wolf, reindeer, hawk owl, willow ptarmigan, pine marten, Amur tiger, northern lights.

Valley of the Giants, Tasmania

Location: Styx valley 55 miles west of Hobart, Tasmania's capital.

Area: 58 square miles (as proposed by the Wilderness Society of Australia and Greenpeace for a future Styx 'Valley of the Giants' National Park).

Rainfall: 30 to 40 inches.

Temperature: 5°C to 22°C.

Access: Difficult. Styx valley owned by the Tasmanian state government, and logged by Gunns Ltd, the world's largest hardwood woodchip company. Gates on forestry roads often locked.

Look out for: Giant eucalypt, wedge-tailed eagle, white goshawk, wallaby, possum, bandicoot, Tasmanian devil, helicopter dropping napalm – or carrots laced with poison 1080 (to kill the wallabies and possums that threaten seedling plantations).

Californian Kelp Forest

Location: Monterey Bay National Marine
Sanctuary, Central California, south of San
Francisco, between Marin and Cambria.
Area: 276 miles of shoreline and 5,322
square miles of ocean. Deepest point 10,663
feet (more than 2 miles). Distance out into
the Pacific ocean, about 30 miles.
Average sea temperature: About 13°C.
Access: By boat along permitted corridors,
and by snorkel and aqualung.
Look out for: Giant kelp, sea otters, harbour
seals, sea anemones, dolphins, whales.

Mediterrean Maquis and Garigue

Location: The olive belt of the Mediterranean
littoral.
Rainfall: About 15 inches.
Temperature: Near-freezing to 28°C.
Access: To *maquis*, sometimes difficult, ˙
because of dense, spiny shrubs. The more
open *garigue* is easier to explore.
Look out for: Evergreen oak, thorny broom,
myrtle, strawberry tree, box, lentisc, thyme,
juniper (*maquis*), rock rose, iris, crocus,
jonquil, orchid, helleborine (*garigue*).

Petrified Forest National Park of Arizona

Location: Northern Arizona, about 55 miles west of the New Mexico border and 25 miles east of Holbrook. The main park road (28 miles) runs north/south through the park, from milepost 311 on Interstate 40, to US Highway 180 at south end.

Area: 93,533 acres

Rainfall: 8 inches (most of it in July as thunderstorms).

Temperature: 10°C (night) to 35°C (day) in summer.

Access: Open all the year round except Christmas day. $10 vehicle fee, $5 walk-in.

Look out for: Coloured, fossilised logs of the Chinle formation, pronghorn, desert cottontail, rattlesnake.

Sherwood Forest

Location: Between Nottingham and Worksop, mainly west of A614.

Area: in medieval times, about 140 square miles of heathland, with 15 areas of dense woodland, mainly oak and birch.

Rainfall: 24 inches.

Temperature: From below freezing to 21°C.

Access: Sherwood Forest Country Park and Visitor Centre, just north of village of Edwinstowe on B6034. Park open daily, dawn to dusk.

Look out for: The Major Oak (20-minute walk from visitor centre along surfaced paths), estimated weight 223 tons, spread of branches 92 feet, estimated age 800 years.

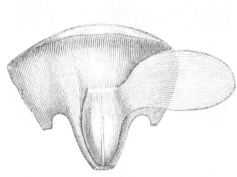

Fig. 3387. — *Agathis (Dammara) australis.* Bractée et écaille connées du cône, la dernière portant sur le milieu de sa face inférieure le fruit unique renversé et pourvu d'....

Kauri Pine Forests of New Zealand

Location: in North Island, from the North Cape for about 250 miles south past Auckland, on the western side.

Area: Waipoua Forest Sanctuary near Dargaville, about 80 miles north west of Auckland, is 22,500 acres.

Rainfall: 50 to 80 inches

Temperature: 5 to 25°C. Average in summer (Dec-March) 19°C; in winter (June to September) 11.6°C.

Access (to Waipoua): From State Highway 12, along boardwalks and tracks to principal kauris ('Tane Mahuta' only 5 minutes from road). Longer tramping tracks into the forest interior. No dogs. Information at Waipoua Forest Visitor Centre at Dargaville.

Look out for: 'Tane Mahuta', 'Lord of the Forest', (height 170 feet, girth 45 feet); kiwi bird, kakako, red-crowned parakeet, weta, kauri snail, orchids, filmy fern, kauri grass.

Baobab Woods of Madagascar

Location: Western Madagascar.

Distribution: 6 endemic species scattered throughout region.

Rainfall: 38 inches.

Temperature: 20°C to 35°C.

Access: Bush taxi from Morondava.

Look out for: Baobab Alley (stands of *Adansonia grandidieri*) near Morondava; pollinating lemurs.

Canada's Great Bear Rainforest

Location: The Pacific coast of British Columbia, from the top of Vancouver island to the Alaskan panhandle.

Area: 27,000 square miles.

Rainfall: 80 to 150 inches.

Temperature: Near-freezing to 15°C.

Access: By sea or along backpackers' trails.

Look out for: Douglas fir, sitka spruce, western hemlock, western red cedar, salmon, kermode spirit bear, grizzly bear, eagle, wolf, deer, wild goat, flying squirrel, marbled murrelet.

Ancient Rainforest of the Cape York Peninsula

Location: North of the town of Coen, between McIlwraith and Iron mountain ranges.

Area: About 2,000 square miles.

Rainfall: 80 to 315 inches.

Temperature: 20 to 35°C.

Access: North of Lockhart River, bushwalking and camping (subject to permit) allowed in limited area of forest with Queensland National Park status.

Look out for: Buff alder, silkwood, crowsfoot elm, strangler fig, orchid, giant tree frog, golden bower-bird, black cassowary.

Acknowledgements

Grateful acknowledgement is made to the following sources and photographers for permission to reproduce their photographs on the following pages:

Art Directors and Trip: 16 (W. Jacobs); 21, 26-7 (A. Wright); 56-7 (M. Jelliffe); 60, 61 (O. Semenenko); 64 (S. Ishakov); 70-1 (O. Semenenko); 76 (Robin Smith); 98-9 (Bob Turner); 102-3 (TH-Foto Werbung); 104 (Viesti Collection); 108-9 (Jerry Dennis); 110, 111, 116-7, 120 (Gordon Gadsby); 123, 125, 131 (W. Jacobs); 142 (Twink Carter); 150-1 (J. Pugh); 153 (M. Both); Endpapers (Ron Bambridge)

Auscape/Jean-Paul Ferrero: 127; 152; 155; 156-7

Corbis: 135 (Yann Arthus-Bertrand)

Gertrud and Helmut Denzau: 30, 31, 33, 34, 37, 39

FLPA: 51 (Rodger Tidman)

Lastrefuge.co.uk: 81 (Adrian Warren); 113 (John Waters); 160-1, 162, 164 (Adrian Warren)

Mary Evans Picture Library: 169 left

Natural History Museum, London: 167 right; 171 left; 173 right

Naturepl.com: 4-5 (Juan Manuel Borrero); 10 (Staffan Widstrand); 20 (Paul Hobson); 40 (Francois Savigny); 47 (Morley Read); 49 (Staffan Widstrand); 66-7 (Andrey Zvoznikov); 72 (John Cancalosi); 74-5 (Dave Watts); 82 (Jeff Rotman); 83 (Georgette Douwma); 85, 88-9 (Jeff Rotman); 93 (Jose Ruiz); 100 (John Cancalosi)

Oxford Scientific Films: 3 (Richards Herrmann); 11 (Michael Fogden); 22 (Niall Benvie); 41, 42, 44 (Michael Fogden); 63 (Konrad Wothe/SAL); 114 (Ronald Toms); 122 (Konrad Wothe); 132; 143 (Rodger Jackman)

Royal Botanic Gardens, Kew: 167 left; 168; 169 right; 170 left; 171 right; 172 right; 173 left; 174 left; 174 right

Royal Geographical Society Picture Library: 170 right; 172 left

Still Pictures: 13 (Michel Roggo); 14 (Claus Meyer); 50 (J-L &M-L Klein-Hubert); 53 (M.C. Thouvenin); 58 (Cyril Ruoso); 73 (J-L & M-L Klein-Hubert); 86 (Bob Evans); 92 (Marc Duquet); 94 (Jean-Jacques Alcalay); 101 (John Cancalosi); 107 (Jean-Pierre Silvestre); 133 (UNEP); 136 (Olivier Langrand); 138-9 (Martin Harvey); 144 (Charlie Russell); 149 (Muriel Hazan)

First published in the
United Kingdom in 2004
by Weidenfeld & Nicolson
The Orion Publishing Group
Wellington House
125 Strand
London WC2R 0BB

Printed and bound in Italy by Printer Trento and
Lego Vicenza.

A CIP catalogue record for this book is available from
the British Library.

A Here+There book for Weidenfeld & Nicolson
Art Direction: Caz Hildebrand
Design: Julie Martin
Picture Editor: Lily Richards
Editor: Joe Dolce
Copy Editor: Chris Knutsen

www.hereandtheregroup.com

Page 3: Giant kelp (*Macrocystis pyrifera*), Catalina
Island, California.